Trouble at the Sandbox

By Phillip Simpson

Illustrated by Leigh Hedstrom

CONTENTS

CHAPTER 1

The Sandbox

It was hot in the Sandbox. *Really* hot. It didn't matter, though. Theo was with his friends, Izzy and Josh.

There was a big sun shade over the sandbox area, which helped. They also had their hats on, so it wasn't so bad.

Theo had his drink bottle nearby.
It was important to drink lots of water
when it was hot.

Theo and his friends spent every
lunch time in the sandbox.

Sometimes other kids would join them.
But most of the time, they had it to
themselves. Theo didn't mind sharing, but
it was better when they had more room.
More room to build things out of sand.

Today, they were making a volcano.

Izzy had started it, and already it was *huge*. Josh and Theo were helping her. They had a couple of the big toy trucks.

Izzy dug out the sand with a plastic spade. She was making a river for the volcano. As she dug, Theo and Josh loaded the trucks up with sand. They put the sand in a big pile at the far end of the sandbox.

Theo dropped off a load of sand and came back for some more. Josh and Izzy helped him load up his truck.

As they were doing this, a long shadow blocked out the light. Theo looked up. A tall boy stood over them. They'd seen him around. He was a couple of years older than Theo and his friends. Two other large boys stood behind him.

CHAPTER 2

The Trucks

"Hi," Theo said. "Do you want to play in the sandbox too?"

The big boy laughed, but it was a mean laugh. It made Theo feel a little scared.

"No," he said. "We want your trucks."

"Wha...what?" Theo replied. Why did he want *their* trucks? They were playing with them.

Without the trucks, they wouldn't be able to build their volcano.

"But we need them," said Josh.

"I don't care," said the big boy. He put his hands on his hips. "We want them, and we're taking them."

He and his friends stepped forward. Theo tried to stop the boy from taking the truck he was using. But the boy was much too big and strong for Theo.

One of the big boy's friends got the truck from Josh. Josh looked like he was going to cry.

The big boys walked off, carrying the trucks under their arms. Theo and his friends watched them go.

"What are we going to do *now?*" asked Izzy.

Theo was too upset to answer at first. Then he thought about it. There was only one thing to do. Go and find a teacher. A teacher would sort this out.

CHAPTER 3
Ms. Lee

Ms. Lee was sitting at her desk when the boys ran into the classroom.

"Ms. Lee, Ms. Lee, there are these boys and they've ..." Theo began.

Ms. Lee held up one hand to stop him.

"Theo," she said with her soft voice. "Take a deep breath and calm down first. Then you can tell me the whole story."

Theo liked Ms. Lee. She was kind and always listened when he had a problem. She was always smiling. Theo did what she said. He took a deep breath and then another one, just to be on the safe side.

He started telling her what had happened.

"Do you know who these boys are?" she asked.

Theo shook his head. "I don't know their names. We could show you who they are, though."

10

"Okay," Ms. Lee said. "Show me."

They searched *all* over the school. They couldn't find the big boys.

"Don't worry," said Ms. Lee. "We'll sort this out. What should you do if this happens again?"

"Come and tell you?"

Ms. Lee nodded. "That's right. If it happens again, you come and find me."

Ms. Lee walked Theo, Izzy, and Josh back to the sandbox and left.

CHAPTER 4

The Volcano

There was no one else in the sandbox. Their volcano was still there, unfinished.

Theo and his friends had *work* to do. Without the trucks it would be hard, but they could still finish it.

They set to work, but soon enough, the bell rang.

"Oh, well," Theo shrugged. "Guess we'll finish it tomorrow." Izzy smiled. Josh still looked upset as they ran back to the classroom.

***

At lunchtime the next day, Theo and his friends went back to the sandbox. There was no one else there. The trucks were there, though. The big boys must have put them back.

The volcano was still half-finished.

"Awesome!" said Izzy. "Let's get straight to work."

They took turns digging out the sand and dumping it into the trucks.

Izzy finished the river, and Josh took one of the trucks to the water faucets.

He came back with the truck filled with water. Izzy and Theo tipped the water into the moat.

They were just finishing the volcano when Theo heard steps behind him. He looked up and his heart sank. It was the big boy *again* with his friends.

14

CHAPTER 5

Lights, Camera, Action!

The big boy looked at Theo. He wasn't smiling. "We need your trucks again."

"You can't have them," Theo said bravely. "Ms. Lee said so."

"Too bad," said the big boy. "We need them."

He looked back at his two friends. They grabbed the trucks out of Josh's and Izzy's hands.

"We'll tell Ms. Lee," said Izzy.

The big boy shrugged. They walked off with the trucks.

Theo, Josh, and Izzy ran to tell Ms. Lee. This time, she was clearly mad. Her eyes got smaller when she was angry.

"We'll see about *this*," she said. "Let's go."

Theo and his friends hurried to keep up with Ms. Lee. They searched all over. Once again, they couldn't find the big boys.

Ms. Lee went to the staff room. She told Theo and his friends to wait outside. When she came back out, she didn't look angry anymore.

"I know where your trucks are," she said. "Follow me."

Ms. Lee led them to another classroom.

16

It was one of the middle school classrooms where the big kids were.

Theo, Izzy, and Josh followed her inside. It looked like a movie set. There were lights set up and a camera. The camera was pointed at a painted background. The background looked like a quarry or mining pit.

At the front were two trucks. The trucks from the sandbox.

The three big boys were there. So was their teacher, Mr. Park. They all looked up when Ms. Lee walked in.

"Mr. Park," said Ms. Lee. "We seem to have a problem here."

"Yes?" said Mr. Park. Theo hadn't had much to do with Mr. Park before, but he looked kind.

CHAPTER 6

Ms. Lee and Mr. Park

"Some of your boys have been taking toys from my kids without asking," said Ms. Lee. "I don't think this is very fair *or* very nice."

Mr. Park smiled. He had a nice smile.

"Oh, sorry, Ms. Lee. I asked my boys to get some trucks for this movie we're making. I didn't mean for them to take toys from other children."

He looked at the big boys. They didn't look very happy.

"Ben, I think you have something to say," said Mr. Park.

The big boy looked at his feet. He didn't seem scary anymore. It was probably because the teachers were around.

"Sorry," he mumbled.

"We didn't hear that properly," said Mr. Park.

"Sorry," he said, lifting his head and looking Theo in the eye.

Mr. Park nodded. He looked at Ms. Lee.

"I'll tell you what," said Mr. Park, "I need some more help with the movie. Do you think I can borrow your students?"

"Of course," said Ms. Lee. "That is, if they *want* to help."

Theo, Josh, and Izzy all nodded their heads. Of course they wanted to help. Making a movie! How cool was that!

CHAPTER 7

The New Volcano

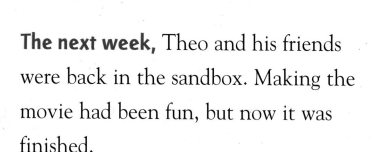

The next week, Theo and his friends were back in the sandbox. Making the movie had been fun, but now it was finished.

It turned out the big boys weren't so bad after all. The trucks were back again. They were making another volcano, and this time it was going to be even *bigger!*

They had only just started when a shadow fell over Theo again. He looked up and saw Ben. Theo's heart sank. "Not again," he thought.

He was about to get up and run and
tell Ms. Lee. Then Ben smiled.

"That looks like fun," he said.

Theo smiled back at him. "It is,"
he said.

"I thought you guys could use a hand," said Ben. "Mind if I help?"

Theo picked up one of the trucks and handed it to him. "We need some sand moved over there," Theo said, pointing to a corner.

Ben nodded and started loading the truck. They all got to work. They had *lots* to do if this volcano was going to be better than the last.